A National Trust Series for Children

# Ghost Hunters

## THE INSIDE STORY OF HAUNTED HOUSES

Harry T Sutton

*Simon Garland*

# BATSFORD-HERITAGE BOOKS

Research: R J Sutton

Design and art direction: Fetherstonhaugh Associates, London

Illustrations: Chapters 1 and 2, Chris Molan; Chapter 3, Liz Elmhirst and Valerie Headland

Copyright © 1978 by B T Batsford Limited and Heritage Books

Produced by Heritage Books

Published jointly by B T Batsford Limited and Heritage Books

Distributed by B T Batsford Limited, 4 Fitzhardinge Street, London W1H 0AH

Printed by Robert MacLehose & Co. Ltd, Glasgow

ISBN 0 7134 1729 3

# Contents

# 1 The Phantom in the Cellar

'Not all ghosts are bad, you know,' said the Colonel. 'I once heard about a ghost which was quite the opposite. It saved some children from almost certain death!'

We were sitting round the fire on a cold December night – it was Christmas Eve, just the time for ghost stories – and we all begged the Colonel to tell us about the good ghost.

'It's a bit creepy,' he warned us. 'Don't want to have you waking up at night and imagining things do we?'

The Colonel was a sort of uncle, not a real relative but a friend of the family who came to stay at times like Easter and Christmas. Usually when he told us stories his eyes had a little twinkle which was a sign that he was making it all up as he went along. And he was very good at making up stories. But this time there was no twinkle in his eyes as he began the

story of the good ghost. He looked very serious and we could see that the story this time must be true.

'It is usual,' began the Colonel, 'for ghosts to appear in dark places. Underground passages, graveyards at dead of night – that sort of thing. But this ghost, which my grandfather saw when he was a child – this ghost appeared in broad daylight. It appeared, moreover, in a very ordinary place – a back garden in London. Behind a small house in Chelsea.'

The Colonel bent forward in his chair to be closer to the fire and we all moved a little closer too. For the room seemed to have a chilly feel, which we had not noticed before.

'My grandfather, with his brother and two sisters, had moved to London from the country,' the Colonel went on. 'Their mother had just died and, left alone with four children, their father thought that a small house in London near his place of work, would be easier to manage. All this happened a fair time ago, of course. It was in the year 1910, when my grandfather was only twelve years old.

'The children liked their new house very much but after living in the country they knew that they would miss the fields and trees. So it was natural that the first thing they did was run out into the back garden to see how big it was and what sort of games they could play. You can imagine their excitement. The garden was very overgrown for the house had been empty for months. They dashed about, calling out to each other the things they found: "There's an old rockery under all these nettles!" "It looks as though there's been a lilypond. Perhaps we can fill it up and get some goldfish!" "We can keep our bikes in this old shed!"

'One of the boys had gone right down to the end of the garden and there he found something really exciting. "There's some steps!" he shouted. "I can see a sort of trap-door at the bottom!"

'Excitedly, the four children gathered at the top of a little flight of stone steps and gazed down at a round wooden door which fitted into a brickwork frame. There was an iron ring at one side and hinges at the other. "Let's open it!" suggested one of the children. "It may lead to a secret underground

passage!" "Or to a cellar with hidden treasure!" '

The Colonel paused at this moment and looked very seriously round at us.

'It was now that the thing happened which makes this such a very strange tale,' he said. 'You see, the children had just started down the steps. They were halfway down, in fact, when suddenly, in front of them, standing exactly over the trap-door – they saw their mother! She held both her hands stretched out in front of her as though imploring them to go no further! "Go back! Go back!" she seemed to be saying. Although no words came from her mouth.'

The Colonel paused again for a moment and looked into the fire.

'My grandfather, even though it was years later when he told me about it, was still very moved by the memory. "We children were scared," he said. "Why, we had been to our poor mother's funeral only a few months earlier. Yet here she was, looking real – not a bit like a ghost – telling us not to run down those steps!"

'Well,' concluded the Colonel, 'the upshot was that the children ran terrified back to the house to tell their father what they had seen and he did not believe them at first. He told them they should not make up tales about their poor mother, especially so soon after her death. But he was soon to change his tune!'

The Colonel paused, his bronzed face sharply outlined by the flickering firelight, and when he spoke again, his voice was quiet:

'You see,' he said, 'next day, the family dog, a beautiful labrador retriever, also explored the garden. He also went to those steps but he ran down them – and did not stop in time. He jumped straight on to the trap-door – and fell right through it for the wood was rotten. Underneath there was a deep well.

'They had a hard time getting the poor dog out. He was drowned, of course.'


That story got us really interested in ghosts and hauntings and when a few days later our Colonel friend told us he was to go on a ghost hunt, we asked if we could go as well.

'Just a moment,' said the Colonel. 'You had better hear what we are to hunt for first. You may not want to come when you know more about it!' We all fell silent for the tale of the Ghost in the Garden was still fresh in our minds and that was scary enough.

'Please tell us,' said my sister, at last. 'We are not afraid of ghosts.'

But her voice did not sound very brave.

The Colonel smiled.

'Very well then,' he said. 'The haunted house is in this very town and I have just this morning had a letter asking if I would like to spend a night in it – tonight, in fact – to see if we can get to the bottom of some very strange goings-on.'

He paused, and when he spoke again he was deadly serious.

'It is a detached house in about an acre of land. Four bedrooms on the first floor, three bedrooms, servants' rooms, and a boxroom above and the usual hall, sitting-room, dining-room and kitchen downstairs. Oh, and there's a big cellar. And that seems to be the centre of the haunting.'

'Is it an old house, Colonel?' I asked.

'Built in the 'twenties I should say. But the cellar is much, much older. Could be any age – 1300, 1500; it's difficult to date it even approximately, but it was certainly part of a much earlier building on the same site. Perhaps a monastery pulled down in the time of Henry VIII. Or it could have been a medieval inn. Whatever it was, it seems that the ghost is of a hooded monk who has been left behind in the cellar which is the only bit of his old home where he can still live!'

The Colonel laughed and for a moment the twinkle came back into his eyes. But then he became serious again.

'The owners will not live in the house. Nobody will rent it. So it stays empty. The ghost has it to himself.'

'What does it do?' I asked. 'The ghost?'

'Oh,' replied the Colonel. 'Moves things about. Makes rapping noises. And sometimes it appears – a hooded monk, coming up out of the cellar and wandering about the house.'

He looked round at us for a moment, smiling. Then he said: 'It seems that just before the ghostly monk appears, the air temperature drops suddenly. It becomes chilly on the warmest nights. Anybody still want to spend the night there with me?'

There was a silence at this. But then I heard myself saying: 'I'd like to come please, Colonel!', and almost as soon as I had said it, I wished I had not.

'Well done!' the Colonel said to me. 'You're the eldest – thirteen now aren't you? – so it is right that you should help me hunt the ghost.'

There was a hush as my brother and two sisters looked at me with new respect.

'We shall set off after supper – say 8.30,' said the Colonel. 'I shall take my revolver with me – loaded. Just in case there is somebody playing the fool. You had better bring a torch. And wrap up warm!'

The 'haunted' house was exactly as the Colonel had described

it – standing back from the road, empty and derelict. There were five of us in the ghost hunting party. The Colonel, a friend of his who was a member of the local Society for Psychical Research – his name was Smith – myself and two young men on vacation from university. One was called John, the other Bill. There was also the Colonel's dog, Sausage, a fat little overfed dachshund.

'Dogs can often see things invisible to us,' said the Colonel. 'Sausage will be extremely useful I'm sure.' But it seemed to me that Sausage was the most frightened one amongst us. He was certainly the fattest!

Mr Smith, who had planned the ghost hunt, had the key for the front door and he let us in to the gloomiest entrance hall I had ever seen. There was damp everywhere. The wallpaper was hanging down in strips; there were thick cobwebs between the banisters of the staircase; part of the ceiling had fallen at some time and there was a pile of broken plaster on the tiled floor. When the Colonel slammed the front door behind us, the noise of its closing echoed with the hollow sound of a house empty of furniture, floors bare of carpets and windows without curtains.

Bill shivered. 'Ugh!' he said, 'the ghost is welcome to live here!'

'Wait until you see where the poor thing apparently spends its time,' said Mr Smith, and opening the door to the cellar, he led us down some stone steps which stretched into inky darkness below.

Lit only by electric torches which each of us held, the place was more like a tomb than the cellar of a suburban house. The roof was of arched brick, covered in green slime at one place where water from above seeped through. Along each side there was a built-up platform or shelf.

'For wine stocks I expect,' said Mr Smith.

'Or coffins,' said the Colonel.

I was very glad when we left the cellar and Mr Smith allotted to each of us a watching-place for the night. John and Bill were to stay in the entrance hall to watch the cellar door. Mr Smith and I were to be together on the first-floor landing and the

Colonel was to sit in one of the two bedrooms on the floor above. 'They were the maids' bedrooms,' Mr Smith told him. 'The monk apparently appears quite often in one of them.'

'Not quite the place for a monk,' commented the Colonel. 'Bit of a dirty old monk if you ask me!'

The Colonel's joke was not very much appreciated by us, I'm afraid, for the dank atmosphere of the house was beginning to have a depressing effect upon us all. I was glad to have the company of Mr Smith at my watching-place on the landing and I will admit that when I sat down to wait, I carefully placed myself with my back against the wall. I was not going to have anybody – or anything – creeping up behind me in the dark!

'Everybody quiet now,' Mr Smith called out. 'Listen carefully for noises – footsteps, tapping or creaking of stairs. And if you see anything, shout out so that we all are ready to see it too!'

The house became silent. And we all waited and watched. Outside, I heard a distant clock strike – one – two – three – four – five – six – seven – eight – nine – ten. The ghost hunt had begun.

I had never known such a long night. I heard eleven o'clock strike, then twelve and all the time we stayed absolutely silent and still in the total darkness of the house. Just after midnight, the moon came from behind thick clouds and we could see the staircase leading to the floor above where the Colonel waited, his revolver loaded and no doubt ready to his hand. To the left of us, the banisters sloped down to the entrance hall where the students watched that door which led to the black, damp hole below.

My eyes were just getting accustomed to the welcome moonlight when suddenly there was a noise which made me hold my breath with fear. There was a ghastly sound of bumping and scratching on the stairs above us – and even as we listened in horror the noise grew in strength and came closer. Something – some nameless thing – was COMING DOWN THE STAIRS.

'Your torch quickly!' hissed Mr Smith, and I realised that

he had mislaid his own in the dark.

My eyes glued to the dark outline of the stairs from which the scrabbling noise was still coming, I felt around me for my torch. There it was, just where I had left it! My shaking fingers felt round it for the switch and just as the bumping, scratching noise reached the bottom step, only a yard from where I sat, the beam of welcome light burst from my electric torch and there, caught in its bright circle – was Sausage! Asleep on the top step, he had fallen down the stairs and now, half wagging his tail in belated apology, he waddled his fat way up the stairs again leaving Mr Smith and me laughing in the unfunny way that one does when one's nerves are at breaking point and the pressure is lifted for a moment. Our laughter stopped as quickly as it began. Then there was silence in the house once more as we all resumed our vigil for the ghost.

As we sat on in the dark – for the moon had once more gone behind clouds – it was easy to understand why no one would

live in that sinister old house. Strange noises began soon after we heard that distant clock strike two. Creaking sounds came from the stairs; there was muffled scuffling along the wain-scoting (mice, surely, I told myself); the window on the landing through which we had seen the moon made clicking noises and once I was sure that I heard the sound of tapping on the glass – just as though somebody, or something, was asking to be let in. Once there was a bump and a rattling noise downstairs but when that happened I was relieved to hear John call out: 'Sorry – dropped my blessed torch!'

It was a cold night but we had all put on several layers of clothing to keep warm. It was, in fact, quite comfortable and as the time passed I found it hard to stay awake, despite the creaking stairs and tapping glass. I must have been just dropping off, I think, when suddenly I felt Mr Smith's hand on my arm. He was gripping hard and I could hear his quick breathing as he whispered: 'Wait here – I'm going to investigate!'

I sat up quickly and for the first time that night was really afraid. A current of cold air was blowing down the stairs and from the floor above I could hear – groans. I listened, petrified. Momentarily the groans stopped. There was silence. Then there came the sounds of choking – just as though somebody was being strangled in one of those maids' rooms – just above where I sat, alone on that cold landing!

I could see Mr Smith's torch now, lighting the staircase as he made his way to the upper floor. He had taken off his shoes and was moving silently. I pressed my back hard against the wall and felt the icy chill of that moving current of air sweeping past me. I remembered the Colonel's words: 'Just before the ghostly monk appears, the air temperature suddenly drops!' Could this be the moment we were watching and waiting for? Would the monk come up – or down the stairs?

My mouth felt dry and a cold shiver ran down my spine as Mr Smith reached the top of the stairs and disappeared beyond my sights. The choking had stopped now and the groans had begun again. I found that I had been holding my breath as I strained my ears to detect the faintest sound that might give

warning of the ghostly monk's approach. My lungs were near bursting and my eyes staring wide when suddenly the whole house seemed to burst with noise.

There was a most terrible explosion; a sudden deafening sound which left my ears singing. Then, from the floor above I heard Mr Smith and the Colonel.

'Good God, man!' I heard Mr Smith. 'You might have killed me!'

'If you must creep about without any warning, what can you expect?' came the Colonel's voice. 'I was positive you must be the ghost!'

'But you were asleep – snoring,' declared the angry Mr Smith. 'Snoring and choking to death with every other breath. You terrified the life out of me. And what on earth is this window doing open? No wonder there's an icy draught blowing down the stairs.'

'There's a flat roof outside,' explained the Colonel. 'And Sausage wanted to go out for you-know-what, so I let him out there.'

'But I must say,' the Colonel added, 'I can't understand how I missed you with my revolver. You were very lucky. I'm usually a crack shot. It must have been the torch shining in my eyes.'

I could hear a snort of outrage from Mr Smith and then he came downstairs and sat beside me once more on the landing.

'Blasted amateurs,' I heard him muttering to himself. 'Hunting ghosts with a gun!'

Then the house quietened down again. And the watch went on.

It must have been almost dawn – I had fallen asleep, I'm afraid, just before this – when there was an unearthly yell from the entrance hall below.

'It's him!' I heard.

'It's the monk. Keep him away! Help!'

'Good Lord!' cried Mr Smith. 'They've seen something. And he dashed down the stairs. I followed, and the scene in the hall was one of sheer horror.

John was lying on his back, his eyes staring horribly from

their sockets. The cellar door stood wide open. And Bill was staring at it, a look of abject fear on his face. His hands shook and he was as white as – I almost said as a ghost.

We stood there, not knowing quite what to do when the Colonel came dashing down the stairs, quickly followed by a very frightened Sausage. The Colonel took control at once.

'What's up?' he asked. 'What's he making such a fuss about?' and he pointed to John with a wave of his gun.

'He suddenly gave a yell and said he'd seen the monk,' explained Bill.

'Well?' demanded the Colonel. 'Did you see it too?'

'I – – I *think* so,' replied Bill.

'What do you mean?' asked the Colonel, sharply. 'Either you did see it or you didn't. Which was it?'

'Well,' replied Bill, rather lamely. 'I *think* I saw something.'

The Colonel turned to John who had recovered a little now and was sitting up, wiping his mouth with a handkerchief.

'Come on, stand up,' ordered the Colonel. 'How can we get any sense out of you if you're sitting down there? Right. Now, what happened?'

The young man got unsteadily to his feet.

'It was awful,' he said. 'The ghost came out of the cellar and right up to me. It wore a monk's habit but when it turned and spoke to me – it had no face!'

'Spoke to you!' exclaimed Mr Smith who was getting very interested. 'What did it say?'

'It said – "Follow me",' John told him.

'And did you?'

The student nodded. 'It walked straight through the cellar door but I had to open it to follow.'

'Good Lord,' said the Colonel. 'That really is something.'

'I got halfway down the steps with the ghost leading the way when suddenly – it dispapeared!'

'Well?' demanded Mr Smith, excitedly. 'What then?'

'I turned and ran back here.'

'And yelled the place down,' added the Colonel, not very sympathetically.

And that is all there was to that long night in the haunted house. Later, when we talked about it in the safe, warm sitting-room at home, we decided that John, who said he had seen the monk, must have fallen asleep and had a nightmare. The open cellar door and his story of having followed the ghost down the steps could have just been sleep-walking. He probably woke up when he was halfway down and that would have accounted for him being in such a state of shock.

But then Bill had also claimed to have seen 'something'. Could it perhaps have been just his imagination? It was certainly very unnerving for him, seeing his friend scared out of his wits, shouting: 'It's the monk – keep him away from me!'

Nevertheless, we decided that it must have been a nightmare. And that John had walked in his sleep. But was it? And did he? One thing is quite certain. It gave that young man an awful fright. A few weeks later Mr Smith received a letter from John's mother. 'This is to ask you,' she wrote, 'never again to invite my son to one of your ghost hunts. He has just received the results of his university exams. He has done badly and the reason, I am sure, is that his nerves were badly upset by his night in your haunted house.'

I wonder what those two students really saw . . . ?

# 2 The Inside Story

## THE SUPERNATURAL – WHAT IS IT?

Ordinary life is very ordinary. We get up in the morning; go to school or to work; play games or attend meetings; travel perhaps, a little way home from work or school; eat meals, have baths, sleep. And all the time we are doing these very ordinary things, extraordinary things do not happen. Or do they?

Are there strange events going on all around us that we do not notice because we are busy about other things? That time when you nearly walked in front of a moving bus – did you stop because you looked up from your daydream just in time and saw it coming? Or did some unseen hand hold you back? Did a ghost voice in your ear say – STOP! Was your escape from death natural? Or was it supernatural?

There have always been people to say that ghosts and hauntings are real. Others are not so sure and they try to find out the truth. They are often called ghost-hunters because they go deliberately to haunted houses and places where strange things are said to happen. They call themselves researchers and, in this country, most of them are members of the Society for Psychical Research. The word 'psycho' simply means 'to do with the mind' so psychical research is the study of unusual things to do with the mind – especially apparently supernatural things.

The story described the kind of things that happen when researchers hunt a ghost. Now we can look at what they have discovered and the explanations they give for ghosts and hauntings. From the experiences of the researchers we can find out the 'Inside Story' of the supernatural.

## NOISY GHOSTS

Some ghosts are very badly behaved. They throw things about, ring bells, draw things on walls and make noises like

footsteps or tapping sounds. Because the things they do can be heard, they are called 'poltergeists' which is a German word meaning 'noisy ghosts'. So, for the 'Inside Story', that is what they will be called. Noisy ghosts have been playing tricks on people for centuries. It is possible that even cavemen had noisy ghosts in their caves. The earliest one we know about in England appeared in the year AD 355. People were tipped out of bed, stones were mysteriously thrown about and rapping noises were heard. Nobody could be found responsible so the Devil was blamed.

Modern researchers look for more scientific explanations. Two noisy ghost hauntings happened not long ago which gave researchers some useful clues.

One happened in the United States in Miami in 1967 at the warehouse of a firm which sold novelties and souvenirs. Their goods were stored on high shelves round the sides and down the middle of the room and things kept falling off the shelves and breaking on the floor. This was causing the firm a lot of trouble and the insurance company which had to pay for the losses was anxious to find the cause.

When the owner of the firm first noticed the breakages, he blamed them on to the carelessness of the two clerks who ran the warehouse. He carefully explained to them the need to store the goods well back on the shelves so that they could not be easily knocked down. But as time went on the breakages increased, and boxes of goods right at the back of the shelves would sometimes fall off from a position *behind* other things on the same shelf.

At last the problem became so bad that the owner called in the police who suggested that psychical researchers should be asked to investigate.

The first thing the researchers did was to tell everybody to stand absolutely still every time they heard the crash of something falling. Then they went quickly round and marked the exact position of the fallen article. Next they noted the places where everybody in the warehouse was standing at that time. After several days they found that the same man was always nearest to the noisy ghost whenever it was in action.

This man was one of the two clerks. His name was Julio. His connection with the hauntings was made almost certain when a few weeks later he gave up his job in the warehouse and all the trouble stopped.

The other case of a noisy ghost occurred in Scotland in 1960, and this time a child was the centre of all the trouble.

Eleven-year-old Virginia Campbell had lived all her life on a farm in a very isolated part of Ireland. Then her father decided to give up the farm and move to Scotland. Virginia was sent on ahead to stay with her married brother who lived near Alloa. One November night when she was in bed she heard a 'thunking' noise as though a ball was being bounced in her bedroom. She went downstairs to tell her brother about it, and the noise seemed to go with her. She heard it on the staircase and also on the sitting-room wall. Her brother heard it too but then, when it stopped, he just told her to go back to bed.

The next day, Virginia was sitting in an armchair downstairs when her brother was astonished to see a big sideboard near her begin to move away from the wall into the room. It moved five inches out – then moved back into place again. Soon after this all kinds of strange things happened – and always when Virginia was close by. One day she was ill in bed and the doctor who came to visit her noticed that the linen chest in her room moved more than a foot from the wall; and that there were strange rippling movements running across her pillow.

The next week when Virginia had returned to school, her teacher was surprised to see the lid of her desk apparently forcing itself open even though Virginia was trying desperately to close it. Soon after this a boy, who sat immediately behind Virginia, left his place, and the teacher saw his empty desk lift itself off the floor then slowly sink down again. A few days later Virginia was standing beside the teacher's desk, her hands clasped behind her back, when the heavy desk began to shake violently. Then it turned itself round by more than a foot!

By now, Virginia realised that she was in some strange way

the cause of these hauntings for she turned to her teacher and said: 'Please miss, I'm not trying to do it!'

Virginia's hauntings stopped as suddenly as they had begun. They had, however, been seen by a great number of people and there can be no doubt that they did occur. There was also no doubt that Virginia had been the cause of them. The fact that she was as frightened by her noisy ghost as everybody else must mean that she was not doing it deliberately. It was just something she could not control.

## MAKE A WISH

If noisy ghosts are caused by people moving things about without touching them, the next question is – how does it happen?

The idea that we can make things happen by wishing hard has been believed for a long time. Prayer is one kind of hard wishing and there are very many people who believe that their prayers have been answered in a very special way. A national day of prayer is sometimes called for the recovery of a king or queen who is desperately ill.

Some games players use hard wishing, hoping that it will help them to win. 'Come on, you little beauty,' a golfer will say to his ball rolling across the putting green. 'Run into the hole for papa!' The games player is hoping, not very seriously, that his will power can have an effect upon the golf ball.

Recent tests with dice-throwing have shown that hard wishing almost certainly works – for some people better than others.

A proper study began when a student at an American university told one of his professors that he believed he could influence the way dice fell by simply wishing hard. Dr Rhine, the professor, carried out tests. Two dice were chosen after careful examination to see that they were not weighted in any way, then 562 tests were made, each test consisting of 24 throws of the dice. The same combination of the two dice was wished for all the time and by the end, the student had scored 3,110 correct throws. By the law of averages, he should have succeeded only 2,810 times. The odds against his score

happening by pure chance were 1,000,000,000 to 1. This was clear proof that he was making the dice roll the way he wanted them to, by hard wishing. But only to quite a small extent. His power to do it was really very small.

The fact that the student could make moving dice fall in a certain way was very exciting and it led to many other tests and experiments. Some people proved to be very good at this kind of hard wishing. Uri Geller is probably one of the best known because he has appeared on television. He can, apparently, bend spoons and keys; make stopped watches go, and even deflect the needle of a magnetic compass, simply by wishing hard. In Leningrad, there is a woman who can make matches, cigarettes and pens placed on a table in front they will move. She is also able to pick out colours with the tips of her fingers, when blindfolded. Another person has been found who can actually read a printed page with the tips of her fingers!

An American named Ted Serios discovered that he could make a picture appear on an unexposed film in a camera just by staring into the lens and wishing the picture onto it. Other people have managed to make plants grow more quickly by wishing that they would.

# HOW IT WORKS

Modern scientists use extremely sensitive instruments for measuring electric currents and some of these have now been used to find out more about how human beings 'work'. They have found that we all generate our own electricity, although in tiny amounts. Which should not really be much of a surprise when we already know about some fish, for example the electric eel, which generate so much of it that they can give their enemies a very nasty shock!

We all have a tiny 'electric field' round us which can be measured by the scientists' new instruments and they have found that when people like Uri Geller are using their special powers to move things at a distance, their electric field increases. They are making their own electricity. The woman in Leningrad, who could move matches by hard wishing, made far more electricity than normal people. When she was actually wishing hard, the electric field round her body began to throb in time with the beating of her heart, and she seemed to be able to focus the electric field in the direction of the object she was wishing about. When her hard wishing was over she became very tired as though she had used up a lot of energy. She lost weight too. Her hard wishing was hard work.

Now we can go back and see if these discoveries can be used to explain the noisy ghosts in the warehouse and the house near Alloa. There is one more clue which can help. When the scientists were testing people's electric fields they also discovered that their electric voltage is especially strong when they are upset in some way. When they are angry, excited, or very unhappy. When we get into a blazing temper we can act in very forceful ways. In a very great rage people sometimes throw things about, break toys and slam doors. We 'let off steam' and feel better afterwards.

The belief now is that the people who cause noisy ghosts are letting off steam mentally. They are wishing all the door-slamming and breaking of things – although they do not know that they are. Their electric fields become strong enough to move things at a distance – to make rapping noises and push things off shelves. But only if they are close enough for this unintentional hard wishing to work.

Julio, the warehouse clerk, was a refugee to America from Cuba and he was very unhappy. His unhappiness probably made him angry with the world for making him so lonely away from his family and friends in Cuba.

Virginia, as we know, had been moved from a happy life on a farm in Ireland to a suburb in Scotland where she had no friends. She, also, was very miserable until her family rejoined her in Scotland. Both of them, therefore, could have been letting off steam without knowing it. But people soon get over the worst attacks of anger. They learn to live with their changed situations. This is what happened to Julio and Virginia. They stopped being angry. And their noisy ghosts went away.

## PHANTOM GHOSTS

Noisy ghosts are never seen. They seem to be only bundles of electric energy which can move things about. Phantoms, or apparitions, like the children's mother in the story, are ghosts that *can* be seen. Many people believe that they have seen a phantom ghost at some time in their life, and what these are, and how they happen, is becoming a little better known. The clue may be in 'telepathy' which means passing thoughts from one mind to another. There is a game you can play to test it. You set out a row of playing-cards on a table, six cards will do, then sit with a friend, with the row of cards between you. One of you knows which card is where in the row. The other does not because the cards are face-down. The one that knows the order of the cards now 'wills' the other to pick one of them up – say, the King of Hearts. The best way to do this is by staring hard into the other person's eyes – it is certain to make you both giggle at first. Try hard to pass a mental picture between you. When the one *receiving* the picture gets the feeling of knowing which card to pick up, that is the time to reach out and take it. If you try several times you may find that you both get better and better at it. But then, when the novelty wears off, and you both get rather bored, telepathy will cease to work. That is the usual pattern. You must both

want to succeed and you probably will. It might work as much as seven times out of ten.

Telepathy, or message-passing from one mind to another has been tested by scientists, and they mostly agree that it works. Tests have been done with people several miles apart, and distance does not seem to make much difference. If their two minds are in tune, they can send mental pictures to each other but the power to do so is very weak. The pictures received are rarely exactly like those sent, and quite often the message is not received at all.

Some people believe that telepathy is an ability that we once possessed. Cavemen, because they had no real language could probably make their moods, fears, hopes and intentions known to other cavemen by passing mental pictures. Dogs and cats certainly seem to pass silent messages – we say they have a sixth sense. Perhaps humans have lost the ability because they have learned to talk instead.

There are times, however, when human beings do seem to be able to send mental pictures especially well, and that is when they are faced with great danger, or with death: an

aeroplane pilot faced with a certain crash; a person about to drown. It seems that at this point, people may regain the full power to send mental messages. It may be because of this that people about to die have sometimes been known to appear as phantoms before those they love, or whom they wish to know about their death. Perhaps at a moment of crisis, all our senses, including a sixth sense, are sharpened for one final burst of electric energy, and a mental picture produced then is so strong that it reaches the person for whom it is intended. They believe that they have seen the person sending it. Perhaps they can. But what they are seeing is only another bundle of electrical energy in human shape. All ghosts that people have seen are like shadows. They cannot be felt and they are visible for only a short time. Then, like shadows, they fade away until they can no longer be seen. Perhaps the mental image runs out of electrical energy.

That explanation is quite a good one for 'crisis' ghosts. But there are also ghosts which are said to appear regularly, and there are stories about some of these in the next chapter. The 'Inside Story' of these may be that some bundles of electric energy, if they were strong enough in the first instance, do not fade away quite so quickly so that they may become visible again from time to time. Then, as time passes, the store of energy becomes weaker until at last they are no longer strong enough to be received by our 'sixth sense' at all. The haunted house, or castle battlement, is haunted no longer. We say that the ghost is at rest at last. But perhaps, it has just run out of energy. Its battery has run down!

# 3 Where to see Ghost Haunts

A WARNING TO GHOST HUNTERS

The 'Inside Story', as you can see, is full of ifs and buts. Nobody is able to prove that his explanation for the supernatural is right. Scientists can still only say: 'The most likely explanation is . . .' But they are still not absolutely sure. Meanwhile serious study into ghosts and hauntings goes on and one day, perhaps, we shall know the full 'Inside Story'.

Until then, it is best not to try ghost hunting or, like the Colonel and the students in the story, you may scare yourself stiff. An American writer named James Thurbur put it very well.

'Leave your mind alone,' he said.

Whatever the truth about ghosts, there is no doubt that we all like a good ghost story whether we believe in them or not. Some people say that Britain has more haunted places than any other country in the world. We certainly have a large number. People have reported seeing ghosts in nearly every kind of place you can think of – from bungalows and village pubs to stately mansions and ancient castles. There are even modern ghosts like that of the racing driver complete with helmet and goggles which is supposed to haunt the old race-track at Brooklands near Weybridge in Surrey.

Of all these stories perhaps the most dramatic are those connected with the old country houses and castles of Britain. Here are the very best tales of headless monks and ghostly coaches, beautiful phantom ladies and mysterious midnight visitors. These are stories which make you draw a little closer to the fire when they are told. Here now is a selection of National Trust properties which are supposed to be haunted. Who knows, you might even see one of them yourself!

# BUCKINGHAMSHIRE
## Claydon House
There are several ghosts at Claydon. The most famous is that of Sir Edmund Verney. He was King Charles I's standard bearer at the Battle of Edgehill. When he was surrounded by the enemy he refused to surrender the standard. The Roundheads killed him but they had to cut off his hand to get the standard because his grip would not relax even in death. After the battle only his hand could be found. It was sent back to Claydon together with a ring and was buried in the family vault. The house Sir Edmund knew no longer exists, but his ghost still wanders around Claydon searching for his lost hand.

When the ballroom was demolished some years ago one of the workmen saw a man wearing strange clothes sadly watching the destruction. When he was spoken to he melted into thin air.

There are also two ghosts in parts of the house not open to the public. On the second flight of the Red Stairs the ghost of a man with a black cloak has been seen. He carried a black hat with a white feather.

In the Rose Room a guest awoke one night to see a beautiful lady dressed in grey standing near his bed. She disappeared into the wall. But this was no ordinary wall. It had once been part of a secret room!

## Hughenden Manor
This house belonged to the great Prime Minister Benjamin Disraeli. He lived during the reign of Queen Victoria. His ghost has been seen several times in the house. Sometimes it appears at the foot of the cellar stairs, at other times in the upper part of the house. Unless he changes his haunt you are unlikely to come across him as these parts of the house are not open to the public.

## West Wycombe Park
Several people are supposed to have seen ghosts here. One poor guest had a shock after dinner one night. He was sitting alone in the dining-room when he suddenly found eleven ghostly figures sitting round the table with him. Noel Coward,

the playwright, was playing a piano in the saloon one evening when he looked up and saw a jolly, smiling monk standing next to him. Then he disappeared. Perhaps he didn't like the music and decided not to stay!

## George and Dragon Inn, West Wycombe Village

The Inn is haunted by the 'White Lady'. Her name was Sukie and she was a serving girl at the Inn in the eighteenth century. She was very pretty and had many admirers, but she was determined to marry a rich gentleman who used to call at the Inn on his travels. Her admirers in the village became jealous and decided to play a trick on her. They sent her a message telling her to be in the West Wycombe caves at midnight dressed in white. Sukie assumed the note was from her rich gentleman and that they were to be married at last. But the tricksters were hiding in the caves. When she got there they jeered at her and tried to make her look a fool. There was a scuffle and Sukie tripped and cracked her head against a stone. The guilty young men carried her back to the Inn but she died in her room before morning. A few days later her ghost appeared in the white dress she had worn at the caves and poor Sukie has haunted the George and Dragon ever since.

## CHESHIRE
### Lyme Park
The Park is haunted by a ghostly funeral procession which winds its way slowly through the grounds. It carries the body of Sir Piers Legh, a medieval knight, who died in France. His body was brought back to the house for burial. Inside the house the Long Gallery (which is sometimes known as the 'Ghost Room') is haunted by a lady in white called Blanche. She loved Sir Piers and died of grief when he was brought back dead to Lyme Park.

## CORNWALL
### Forrabury, nr Boscastle
Local people say you can hear ghostly bells ringing from under the waves near Forrabury. They are meant to come from a ship which sank near the coast. It was carrying new bells for the church.
### St Levan Cliffs, nr Penzance
One clear moonlit night some villagers saw a strange phantom ship at St Levan. It sailed straight towards the coast, right up out of the water and continued inland until it faded away near Porthcurno!

## DEVON
### Buckland Abbey
Sir Francis Drake lived here when he returned from his famous voyage around the world. After the defeat of the Spanish Armada it was said that Drake's victory against such a superior fleet was only possible because he was in league with the devil who summoned up the storms to destroy the Armada. Now on wild and stormy nights Drake's ghost drives a black coach at break-neck speed from Tavistock to Plymouth right past his old home at Buckland. The swaying coach is pulled by black, headless horses with a pack of

headless hounds in front and fiery devils behind. The whole crazy procession dashes along through fields and hedges and over the water to Drake's Island in Plymouth Sound.

## Little Haldon
There is a small area of National Trust land by the side of the road near the village of Little Haldon which is haunted by the Cursed Monk of Haldon. In the fourteenth century he used to rob travellers on this road. When he tried his tricks on a sailor one day he got more than he bargained for. He was thrown down a well! Now the top half of his ghost appears by the side of the road struggling as if to get out of the well.

## HEREFORD AND WORCESTER
## Harvington Hall
In 1710 a woman called Mistress Hicks was hung as a witch at the crossroads near the Hall. Now she haunts the area around the site of her execution.

## KENT
## Scotney Castle
On dark nights a ghostly figure crawls from the castle moat

dripping with dank, stagnant water. It moves towards the great door and knocks on it. Some say it is the phantom of a revenue officer who was killed in a fight with one of the many smugglers who frequented the area. The smugglers threw the body into the moat and now its ghost returns to seek revenge.

## LANCASHIRE
### Rufford Old Hall

Many years ago, during the Scottish Wars, the merry sounds of an engagement party could be heard in Rufford Hall. The bride-to-be was Elizabeth Hesketh, the daughter of the house, and she was to marry a handsome young officer. Suddenly the celebrations were interrupted when word was sent that the Ashurst Beacon was lit. This was the signal for all soldiers to rally and fight the Scots. Elizabeth's fiance had to join them. Some weeks later a messenger arrived to say that the war was won and that the young officer was on his way home safe and sound. The wedding arrangements were started immediately and the sadness at the Hall disappeared. It soon returned as time went by and still Elizabeth's officer had not arrived. Eventually a message was sent to say that he had been killed in the fighting after all. Poor Elizabeth refused to believe it and continued with her wedding plans. She waited and waited, neither eating nor sleeping, until eventually she fell ill and died. To this day her ghost, the Lady in Grey, haunts the house still waiting for the return of her brave young officer.

Not so long ago Mr Ashcroft, who donated the collection displayed in the Hall, saw the Lady in Grey himself. While he was playing the piano in the dining-room one evening he turned round and saw her standing behind him. He continued playing furiously until he had the courage to look round again, but this time the ghost had disappeared!

## LINCOLNSHIRE
### Gunby Hall

Soon after the house was built in 1700 trouble descended on the Massingberd family, the owners. The young mistress of the house fell in love with one of the servants and they decided to elope. Before they could do so the young man was murdered. The story goes that his body was dumped in the pond near the house. As a result a curse was laid upon the family which foretold that no male member of the family would inherit the house. The ghost of the servant is said to haunt the path beside the pond, and it is known as the 'Ghost Walk' to this day.

## LONDON
### Ham House
When all the visitors have left and the midnight hour approaches, Ham House sometimes echoes to the tap, tap, tap of an old lady's walking-stick. She was the Duchess of Lauderdale and she lived here during King Charles II's time. On the terrace behind the house there is a different kind of ghost. It is a cheerful little King Charles Spaniel which is supposed to appear even in daylight. Near the house on the tow-path of the River Thames a mysterious figure in seventeenth-century dress appears. He is said to be a courtier who visited Ham House with King Charles, got drunk and drowned in the river. He has obviously been regretting it ever since!

## NORFOLK
### Blickling Hall
There is a legend that Anne Boleyn lived in the earlier house here when she was a little girl. Later she became Henry VIII's second wife. When she failed to bear him a son she was executed in the Tower of London in May 1536. Now, on the anniversary of her execution, she can be seen, holding her head in her lap, driving towards the Hall in a coach. The coach is pulled by four headless horses and is driven by a headless coachman. When the procession arrives at Blickling it melts away. Anne's brother George was executed at the same time and his ghost has appeared near Blickling too. With his head tucked under his arm he is hauled across the countryside by four headless horses with screaming devils bringing up the rear. It is said that this wild journey must include twelve

bridges crossed before dawn.

## Felbrigg Hall

The ghost here is much more peaceful. In fact, he is rather a scholar. He is the ghost of a previous owner, Mr Windham, and he spends the night looking through his favourite books in the library.

## POWYS

### Powis Castle

The castle has a 'useful' ghost. In the eighteenth century, a local woman was once tricked into sleeping in the castle's haunted room. During the night the ghost appeared and led her to another room. Here it showed her a hidden box. It then told her to send the box to the owner of the castle in London. She did this and the box was found to contain some very valuable documents. As a reward the woman was allowed to stay at the castle free for the rest of her life. The 'useful' ghost still wanders around the castle, so people say.

## SALOP

### Long Mynd, nr Church Stretton

The National Trust owns part of the moors here. Local people say that a phantom funeral procession sometimes appears on them, but there is no story to account for it.

## SUFFOLK

### Thorington Hall

One of the passages upstairs is the haunt of a girl wearing a ghostly brown dress. Strange footsteps have also been heard about the house.

## WARWICKSHIRE

### Charlecote Park

There is supposed to be a ghost in the park at Charlecote. It is the phantom of a young girl who walks towards the water and drowns herself. Nobody knows who she is or why she does it.

# WEST SUSSEX
## Bramber Castle

In 1208 the castle was owned by William de Braose. His children were taken hostage by King John. He kept them prisoner in Windsor Castle and they died of starvation there. Now, especially at Christmas time, the two thin little children are seen gazing at the ruins of their father's castle and begging for food in the streets of Bramber. But if you try to speak to them, they just fade away!

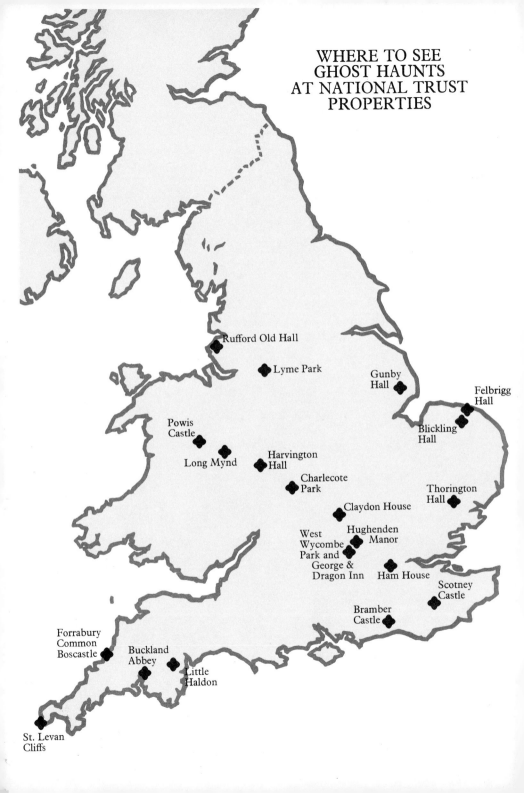

WHERE TO SEE
GHOST HAUNTS
AT NATIONAL TRUST
PROPERTIES

Rufford Old Hall

Lyme Park

Gunby Hall

Felbrigg Hall

Blickling Hall

Powis Castle

Long Mynd

Harvington Hall

Charlecote Park

Thorington Hall

Claydon House

West Wycombe Park and George & Dragon Inn

Hughenden Manor

Ham House

Scotney Castle

Bramber Castle

Forrabury Common Boscastle

Buckland Abbey

Little Haldon

St. Levan Cliffs